Written by:

Sarah Levin Allen, Ph.D. and Kevin Caviston, MBA

Brainy Tales

Illustrated by: Yana Popova

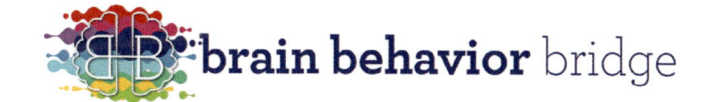

brain behavior bridge

How to use this book: This book is designed to guide you and your children in the discussion of emotions and the brain. After reading the book, scan the QR code below and use the free resources to guide your discussion and grow your child's brain!

Brainy Tales

brain behavior bridge

Text Copyright 2023: Sarah Levin Allen, Ph.D. and Kevin Caviston, MBA

Illustrations: Yana Popova

ISBN: 9-798869804-48-8

All rights reserved under International Copyright Law. Contents and/or cover of this book may not be reproduced in whole or in part in any form without the express written permission of the Publisher/Author.

To our four kids, who challenge our Fronnies and connect us with our Amy G everyday, we couldn't have written this book without you!

Have you ever wondered how your brain works? Yeah? Well, we bet you aren't the only one! Your brain is actually made up of lots of different parts and each one has a different job to do. All of the parts work together to make you... well, you.

Knowing the different parts of the brain and what they do can be really helpful. It can help you understand why you may do certain things when you are happy, sad, excited, or scared.

It can also help you understand why other people do what they do when they have those same feelings.

To help you get to know your brain, we wrote this story about your brain and how it works. We hope you and your brain like it!

My name is Amy G, and people always say I'm sooooo emotional, but I'm supposed to be! Amy G is my nickname.

Hi!

I am named after the **amygdala** (you say it like uh-MIG-duh-luh), the part of the brain that deals with emotions. You know what emotions are, right?

They make you feel happy, sad, angry, excited, and scared...just to name a few. I do my best to handle them, but it's not always easy!

It's hard to deal with emotions, especially when you don't always know why you feel them.

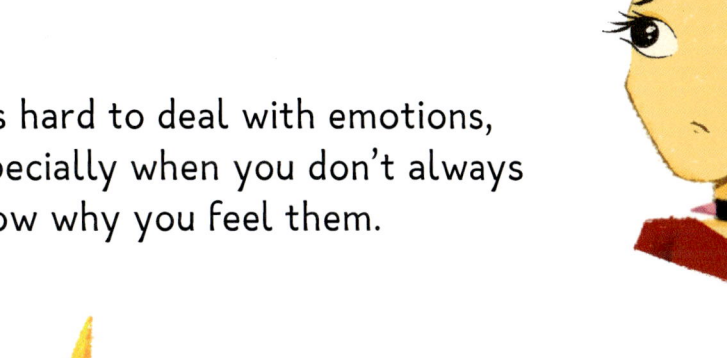

Sometimes, I "puff up" when I have big emotions. But everyday I use my strategies when I experience them. We're all a work in progress, right?

Let's go meet some of my friends at school. It's called Central Nervous School, or CNS for short!

The one greeting the students is Fronnie; she's the school secretary. She has many jobs.

9

Fronnie is named after the **frontal lobe** (you say it like FRUN-tuhl Lowb). It's part of the brain that keeps everything organized and moving.

And that's what Fronnie does here, and boy is there a lot to do. We always have so much going on with all of the students and teachers. They need a lot of help staying on schedule and making sure everything gets done on time.

It's a lot of work, but she's really good at it!

"Hey Hip!" Amy G greets her friend.

Hip the Hippo is my best friend, and I would be lost without them.

But..Hip keeps forgetting they're not an elephant. Let me tell you a secret, it's driving me bonkers! I have to remind them almost every day.

"Wait, what...? I'm not an elephant?" Hip ponders.

"No, you're not, but you are named after the **hippocampus** (you say it like HIP-o-kam-puhs). I'd totally be lost without you," Amy G huffs.

The hippocampus is the part of the brain that's in charge of learning and memory. Clearly Hip is working on this.

"That's right... I am!" exclaims Hip.

"Oh, Hip..."
"I remember now, Amy G. Thanks!" Hip replies with a smile.

"Hey, Mr. BG!" yells Amy G.

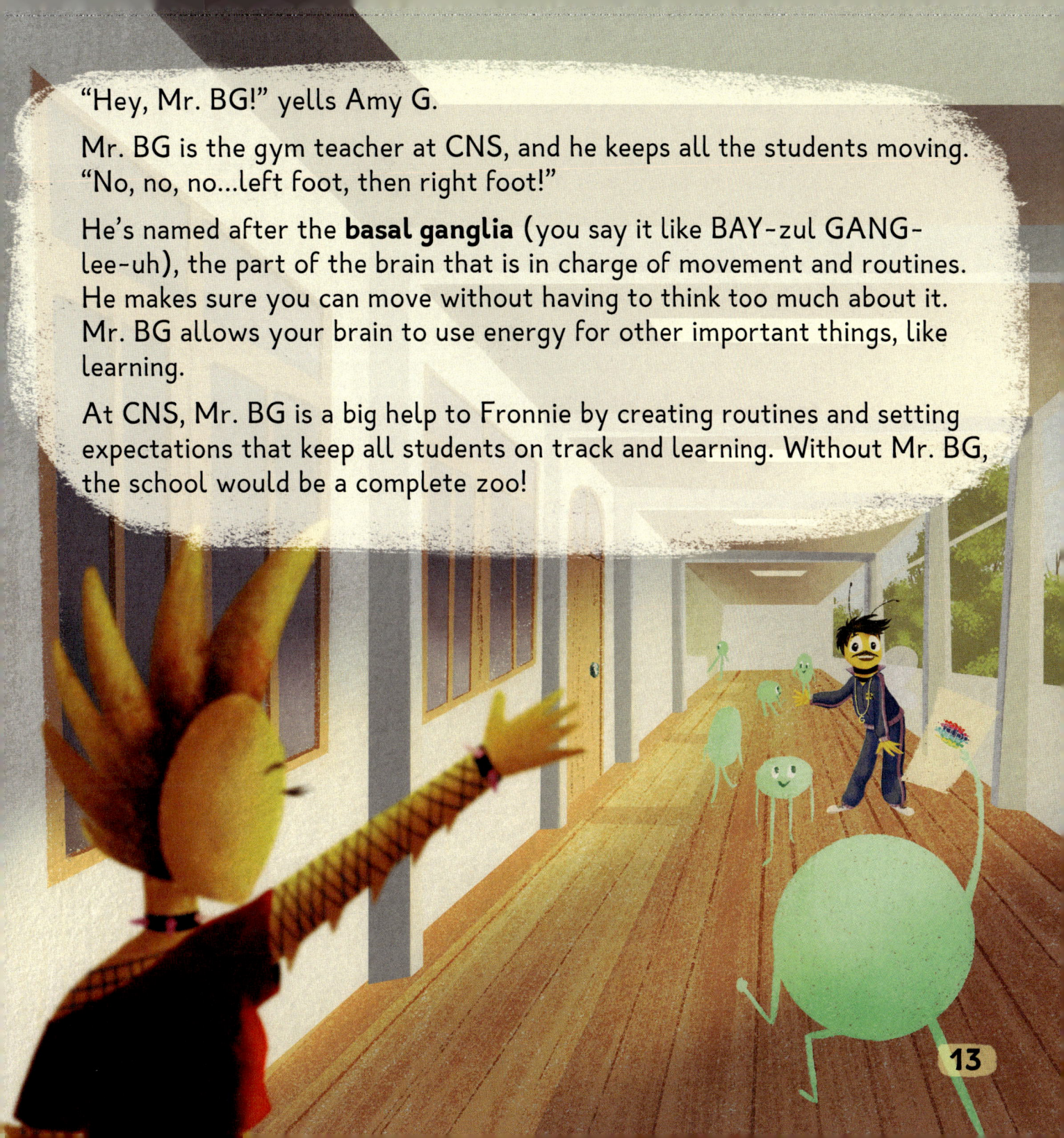

Mr. BG is the gym teacher at CNS, and he keeps all the students moving. "No, no, no...left foot, then right foot!"

He's named after the **basal ganglia** (you say it like BAY-zul GANG-lee-uh), the part of the brain that is in charge of movement and routines. He makes sure you can move without having to think too much about it. Mr. BG allows your brain to use energy for other important things, like learning.

At CNS, Mr. BG is a big help to Fronnie by creating routines and setting expectations that keep all students on track and learning. Without Mr. BG, the school would be a complete zoo!

Hidden in the halls is Thally. He's named after the **thalamus** (you say it like THA-luh-mus), the part of the brain that's in charge of receiving and sending out messages to everyone else.

He runs information technology at CNS. We may not know exactly what he does, but we wouldn't be able to get online without him. He's always around, but we hardly ever see him.

"Bonjour Mrs. P, I didn't see you there."

Mrs. P is the theater teacher here at CNS, and she's named after the **parietal lobe** (you say it like puh-RY-uh-tuhl Lowb). This is part of the brain that's in charge of sensation, touch, and navigation.

"Ah, Amy G, I didn't see you either," she startled. "Are you going on the field trip?"

She's a bit touchy, but she's pretty cool once you get to know her. Especially since she also takes us on hikes for our field trips. She's great at helping us find our way through the woods, but she's always making sure we touch and feel the things around us.

"Yes, I'll be there!" Amy G responds as she makes her way next door.

Amy G hangs in the doorway, "Mr. T, my favorite teacher. You always have the right words to help us understand what we read, hear, and see."

He's named after the **temporal lobe** (you say it like TEM-por-ul Lowb) of the brain, which helps us understand language. Mr. T also allows us to understand what we see and hear.

This makes him a great English teacher! He makes it easier to understand the world around us and always know what's going on at school.

"Oh, Amy G, you always amaze me with how many emotions you know. Your ability to express yourself is quite admirable – but your timing isn't so great! I've a class to get back to," Mr. T grumbles picking up his book.

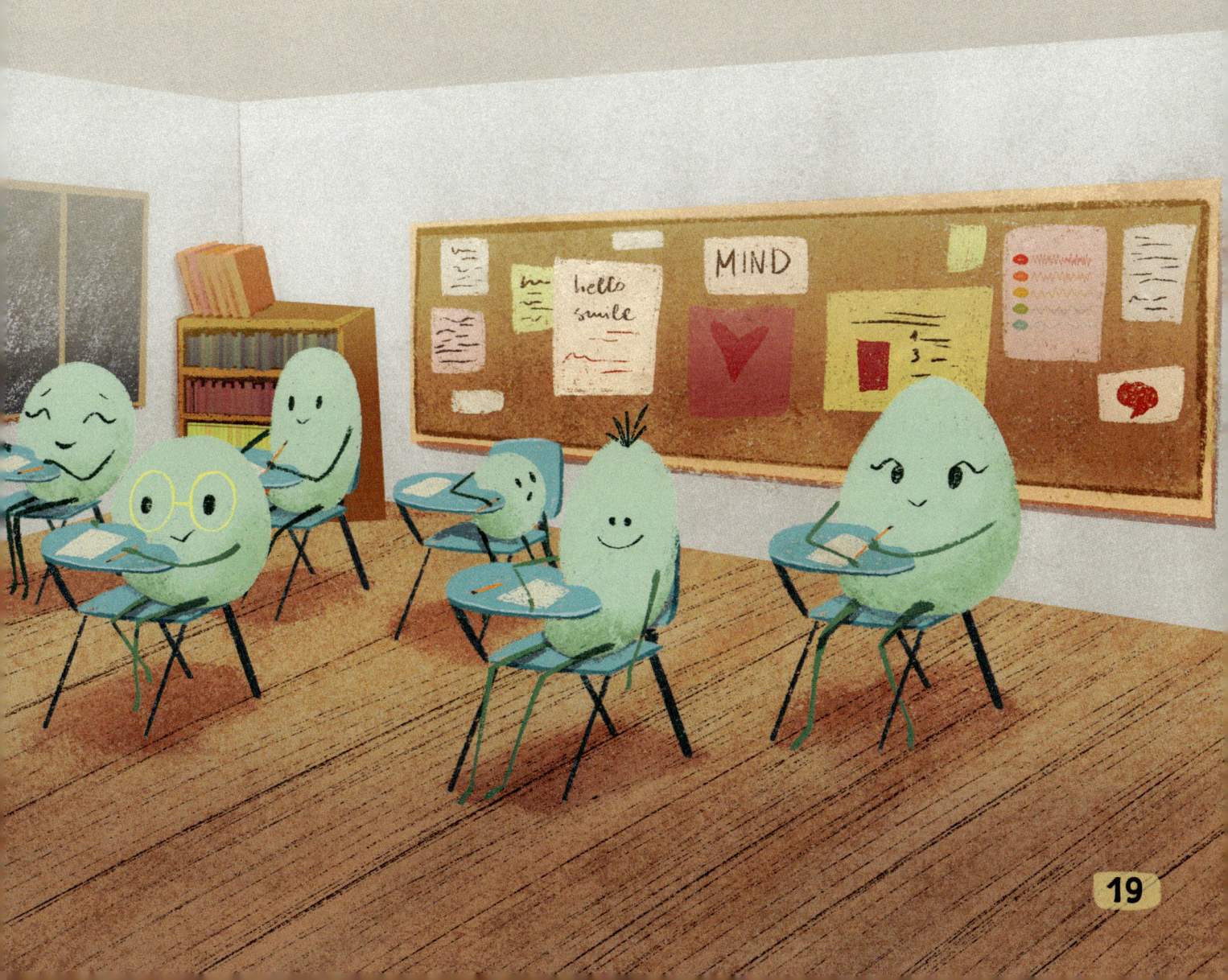

Let's sneak in to see Mrs. OC. She is named after the **occipital lobe** (you say is like aak-SI-puh-tuhl Lowb) of the brain, which is in charge of vision.

It helps you see colors, shapes, and forms! Naturally, Mrs. OC is the art teacher here at CNS.

She teaches us to see things in color and in all sorts of designs.

"Hey, Amy G!"

"Oh, hey there! How did you know it was me?" Amy G squeaks.

"Don't you know I see everything around here?!" Mrs. OC replies with a chuckle.

Amy G laughs in response and turns to go find Hip.

So, that's everyone at CNS. We all come together to make this place work as well as we can.

Sometimes it works great and sometimes...well, not so much. But that's OK.

What's important is that we keep trying to do the best we can. They might annoy me sometimes, but other times they help me.

"Hey, Amy G, like that time you tried to tell me I was a hippo?" Hip says with a side smirk.

Amy G and Hip enter the gym as Amy G puffs up. "You. Are. A. Hippo!!" Amy G shrieks.

As Amy G puffs and screams, Mr. BG decides to get the rest of CNS into their lines. Mr. BG's familiar lines bring a sense of calm over Amy G. Fronnie's only job now is to get Amy G to take a deep breath.

As Fronnie approaches her, Amy G breathes more easily. With her calm breath, Amy G is able to join her friends from CNS.

Fronnie stands across from them.

She took one look at Amy G and Hip and said, "Hip remembers he's a hippo. He's just being a nudge. Remember last time?"

"Breathe."

Amy G takes three more deep breaths and smiles.

She loves when Fronnie helps her calm down.

The three of them join in their line, just like they do when the school gathers in the gym.

I love this place, she thinks. Suddenly, standing with her friends in line makes everything feel right again.

There are four outer parts of the brain called lobes:

frontal lobe (FRUN-tuhl Lowb): The part of the brain that controls our thoughts, behavior, and emotions. This part also plans, organizes, starts us, stops us, and helps us speak out our words.

parietal lobe (puh-RY-uh-tuhl Lowb): The part of the brain that's in charge of sensation, touch, and where you are in your environment.

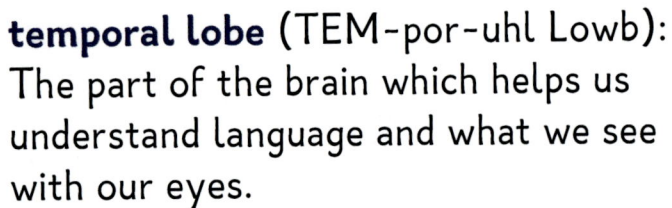

temporal lobe (TEM-por-uhl Lowb): The part of the brain which helps us understand language and what we see with our eyes.

occipital lobe (aak-SI-puh-tuhl Lowb): The part of the brain that's in charge of vision. It helps you see colors, shapes, and forms.

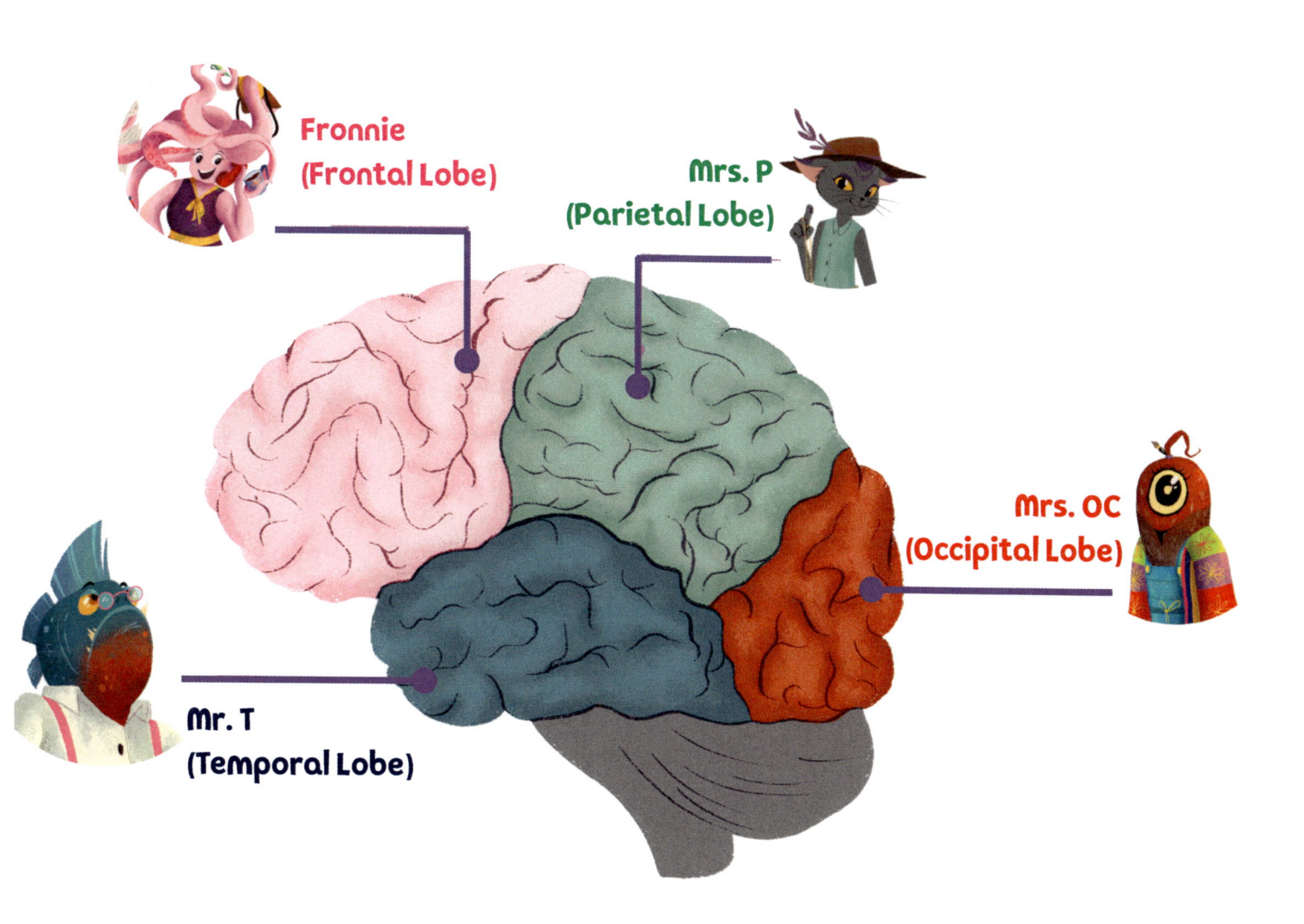

Fronnie
(Frontal Lobe)

Mrs. P
(Parietal Lobe)

Mrs. OC
(Occipital Lobe)

Mr. T
(Temporal Lobe)

There are also parts inside of the brain that are important for our day to day function:

amygdala (uh-MIG-duh-luh): The part of the brain that feels emotions.

hippocampus (HIP-o-kam-puhs): The part of the brain that's in charge of learning and memory.

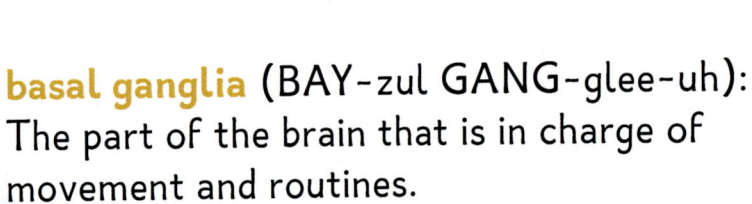

basal ganglia (BAY-zul GANG-glee-uh): The part of the brain that is in charge of movement and routines.

thalamus (THA-luh-mus): The part of the brain that's in charge of receiving and sending out messages about what you see, hear, taste, and touch to the rest of the brain.

**Thally
(Thalamus)**

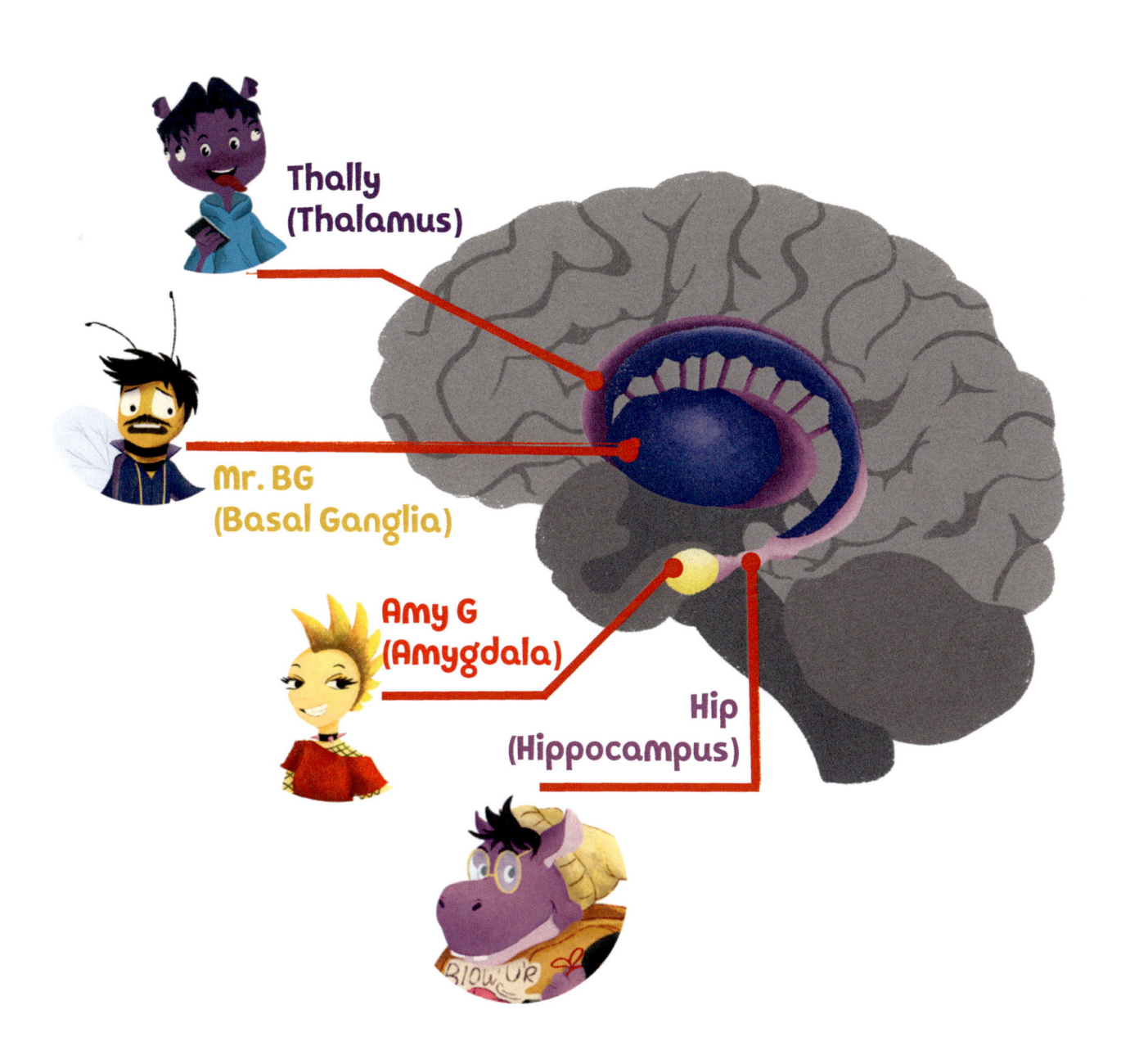

**Mr. BG
(Basal Ganglia)**

**Amy G
(Amygdala)**

**Hip
(Hippocampus)**

About the Authors

Dr. Sarah Allen is an author, pediatric neuropsychologist, parent/teacher strategist, and mom of two bio and two step kiddos. She has more than 15 years experience studying and applying brain science. She is the author of the international bestseller Raising Brains: Mindful Meddling to Raise Successful, Happy, Connected Kids. Dr. Sarah is passionate about helping to raise kids' brains without losing your mind!

Kevin Caviston is an editor, part-time freelance writer, and full-time father of two bio and two step kiddos. Being married to Sarah, he is her partner in crime, her favorite brain student (at least he thinks he is), and a discusser of all things. He's learned to see his own kids as growing brains, which has saved him on many occasions from losing control of his own Amy G!

Morgan Sossa is a teenage artist who created the original designs for Amy G, Fronnie, and Hip. After starting the project, Morgan was diagnosed with a brain tumor and underwent surgery. She used her understanding of the brain parts from this project to inform her recovery. We're excited and appreciative of Morgan's creativity on this project.

Check out BrainBehaviorBridge.com or scan below for actionable tips and resources.

Made in the USA
Middletown, DE
18 February 2025